WE HAVE LOST OUR FATHERS

AND OTHER POEMS

by

Nicholas Rinaldi

A University of Central Florida Book
University Presses of Florida—Orlando

Printed in U.S.A.

We Have Lost Our Fathers and Other Poems, by Nicholas Rinaldi, is published in cooperation with the Associated Writing Programs, and is an AWP Award Series Selection.

University of Central Florida – Contemporary Poetry Series

Other works in the series:

George Bogin: *In a Surf of Strangers*
Van K. Brock: *The Hard Essential Landscape*
Malcolm Glass: *Bone Love*
Susan Hartman: *Dumb Show*
David Posner: *The Sandpipers*
Edmund Skellings: *Heart Attacks*
Edmund Skellings: *Face Value*
Robert Siegel: *In a Pig's Eye*

University Presses of Florida, the agency of the State of Florida's university system for publication of scholarly and creative works, operates under policies adopted by the Board of Regents. Its offices are located at 15 Northwest 15th Street, Gainesville, Florida 32603.

Library of Congress Cataloging in Publication Data

Rinaldi, Nicholas, 1934 -
We have lost our fathers, and other poems.

(University of Central Florida contemporary poetry)
"A University of Central Florida book."
I. Title II. Series: Contemporary poetry series
(Orlando, Fla.)
PS3568.I47W4 811'.54 80-22908
ISBN 0-8130-0692-9

ACKNOWLEDGMENTS

Acknowledgment is given to the following journals for permission to reprint poems they originally published:

Aitia for "She Is Going to Be."
Epoch for "Forbidden Fruit."
International Poetry Review for "Muzak."
The Literary Review for "Shadow of the Crow," "Scenes of Violence," "My Time," "Everything Humanly Possible Was Tried and We Failed %%%%%%%%%%," and "Thomas Edison Considers the Past & the Future and Goes Off in Search of Something Else :::."
O. Ars 2: Perception for "We Have Lost Our Fathers."
Poet Lore for "They."
Southern Humanities Review for "A Vast Silence Arrives in the Sky in the Shape of a Phantom Battleship."
Southern Poetry Review for "The Camel."
Southwest Review for "We Meet/We Part/We Meet Again."
West Hills Review for "Scuba Diver Found Dead in a Swamp."

For My Mother and Father

Contents

Part *1*

Part *2*

Part *3*

. . . in this inner knowledge the thing-in-itself has indeed in great measure thrown off its veil, but still does not yet appear quite naked.

—Schopenhauer

PART *1*

Shadow of the Crow

Gaspari walks beside me, picking at his teeth
with his fingernails. He is older
than I thought. His brown, frayed coat
hangs down to his shoes.

We walk awkwardly, like two brothers
sharing a family secret.
"I can free you from yourself," he says.
"I will relieve you of your burden."

From his pocket he takes the shadow of a crow—
unfolds it, lets it fly.
The shadow races across the sidewalk,
the passing of a sudden cloud.

"Do you feel better now?" he asks.
I don't reply. We face each other,
gazing into the brown emptiness
of each other's eyes.

My disappointment is more for him
than for myself. How well he did that, taking the shadow
from his pocket . . . a noiseless flutter of wings
yearning toward some implausible fulfillment.

"I paid good money for that crow," he says.
Then, wiping his nose with the back of his hand,
he walks off, goes and goes. I had not noticed before
how small his feet are.

Beggars at the Door

We are all hungry, we wait
at the door. We hope someone

will answer. The beast with seven eyes
looks down from a window—

his teeth are black, his face
a raging cloud.

We have come here at the wrong time.
We should have waited.

The beast with seven eyes
grabs us and

rips us apart—tears out our eyes,
breaks our bones.

The beast says: *"Don't come back!"*
But we do. The beast finds us

and feeds us to his dogs—
yet we come back again,

and back again,
because this is the house

where we belong,
and this is the door.

Centenarians

In the Soviet Caucasus, and in Yakutia,
and in the Poltaya district of the Ukraine,
there are people who live
more than a hundred years. They work
out-of-doors: shepherds, beekeepers,
gardeners, carpenters. They eat vegetables and cheese
and not much meat. They have large families.

"I am never in a hurry," says Shirali Mislimov,
holding a shovel. "Don't be
in a hurry to live–this
is the main thing. And one must observe
a daily regimen. I have been doing physical work
for one hundred and fifty years!"

They were born before
my father was born, and some of them
will be alive, working the fields,
long after I am dead. They gather with their children
and their children's children, and they sing,
tell stories, and dance,
and dig the earth, plant trees.
They drink wine. I do not know what prayers they say
when they bury their dead, nor do I know
what kinds of flowers   they bring to the grave.

We Meet / We Part / We Meet Again

Fur hat, straight nose,
long brown skirt hanging far below her knees;
leather boots, red hair tumbling
loose over her shoulders. She is not the person
I thought she was—but adequate, she will do.

"Why do you hate me?" she complains.
"I hate you," I tell her, "because you are part Jewish,
part Puerto Rican, part Irish, and you are not Hungarian!"
She does not smile. "Why do you hate me?" she repeats.
"I hate you," I offer, "because you are the daughter of
a counter-revolutionary fascist who works
for the *New York Times*!" Her eyes are flat,
opaque: dark porcelain covered by a dull glaze.

"Why do you hate me?" she says again.
"I don't hate you," I confess. "I love you!"
And then, oh, she takes a knife
from her black leather boot
and stabs, and stabs,
and I bleed,
and then we go off together, in a park, wondering
what ever happened to
the warm green life
we had imagined
for ourselves.

We Plant Our Feet

First we plant our feet in the ground,
then we hold hands. We shout at the sun.
We tell each other
how miserable we are, we scorn the moon.

We plant our feet, it isn't hard.
You dig a big hole and bury your feet
deep. When your feet are locked in,
you wait for roots to grow.

We plant our feet and tell each other
how glad we are: the sun has not fallen
on our heads. Roots grow, we are planted
firm.

We wait for rain, and wait for snow.
We are lazy in the wind. We plant our feet
and the sound, all around us, is
the sound of waterfalls, an awesome thunder.

Our roots reach down, in stubborn ground,
touching memories, scars,
old horrors of the earth, a lonesome
anger. Something in the sky breaks loose.

We plant our feet, and our roots run
far in the south of our broken dreams:
we lift our eyes, forgetting, and stare
at the sun.

Old Piano

In the barn, where the piano was, my cousin
hammered away at the keys, singing *O Sole Mio*,
and *La Cucaracha*. She was a howler.
Only four and a half feet tall, but seventeen
and hungry for a man, pounding that piano
with all she had, as if it were a magic box that could
make her taller, and more beautiful—and, if she pounded
hard enough, it might open up, abracadabra, giving her
the man she wanted. *Till the End of Time*,
and *Tonight We Love*. "No, no, no," I roared, running
from the barn, and she howled louder than ever.

She found her man, an air-force captain
who flew refueling tankers for the B-52s. He took her
away from the barn, and away from the piano,
and taught her how to fly. They lived in Plattsburg first,
then in Omaha. A quiet man, not tall,
but tall enough to make her four and a half feet
look like four, or less. One day they had him
fly the President's plane
from Dulles International to California,
with the President aboard. It was a wild thrill
for my cousin, being married to a man who for a few hours
had the life of the President
in his hands. The trip was routine, uneventful.
They touched down in fog.

My cousin used to drink gallons of coke;
now she drinks coffee and diet lemonade. She's grown fat

and chews bubble gum. She has three boys.
She doesn't have a piano in the house, but now and then
she hums *O Sole Mio,* and an odd gleam
comes in her eyes: she's in that barn again,
making the dust fly. The beams and the floorboards
vibrate with her rhythm. The piano opens
and the President leaps out, grinning,
and together they take off, full throttle, his life
in her hands: they fly, and fly,
through *The Yellow Rose of Texas* and
Carry Me Back to Old Virginny, and when they touch down
it's in a handsome patch of fog
in a part of the world
she's never seen before, and never will.
That old piano,
they hauled it out to the town dump, the day
they pulled the barn down, clearing the ground
for a supermarket that was going up. Cars come and go—
it's buy and sell. A jet bomber
crosses overhead, leaving a vapor trail. My cousin hums
and mixes lemonade.

The Good and the Bad

There is a chilling moment in *The Good Die Young*
when Robert Morley, playing the father, turns
to Laurence Harvey, playing the son, and says:
"Now I have only one ambition left—to outlive you."
He did, in the movie and in life.

There is another moment in the same movie
when John Ireland, the wronged husband, says
to the man who has wronged him: "All right,
I get the picture. You take what you can get—
and me, I try like hell to keep what's mine!"

Nobody wins in this movie. Four men die.
Laurence Harvey shoots one in the back
and shoves another onto the third rail.
Then he and Richard Basehart
shoot each other in a phone booth.
The money they stole
stays stashed where they hid it,
in a grave.

Refugee Camp

Blue slippers, a broken moon–
where are we now?
Down & down

we fall and nobody helps,
we fall and a dead man rises up in front of us,
        his throat cut, eyes like black glass–
do we escape?

A torn couch to sleep on,
a green moon to make love under,
a purple garden where we forget our memories.

We wait in a slow place where the grass is barbed wire
& we don't move.

Muzak

Muzak in the Pentagon! Muzak in General Motors!
Muzak in the Bank of America and the Bronx Zoo!
Muzak earns $400 million annually. Every day
muzak offers
four programs: industrial, office, public area,
& travel. In a Stuttgart whorehouse, muzak plays
a light industrial program. Muzak has
no words. It shies away
from tunes with emotional identification
& has (in theory) a therapeutic
effect. Cows and chickens who hear muzak
are more productive
than those who don't. Muzak provides
a constantly rising
level of stimulation, varying inversely
with the worker efficiency curve. Muzak belongs
to Teleprompter, which belongs
to ITT.

Pantoum of the Velvet Lake

A yellow taxi drives across the sky,
avocados grow from clouds.
Who can say how or why?
We'd find an answer if we could.

Avocados grow from clouds,
tall aspens wait beneath the moon.
We'd find an answer if we could.
Life is not a gunshot or a stone.

Cold aspens wait beneath the moon,
a wounded grouse dives toward a velvet lake.
Life is not a gunshot or a stone.
We ponder what we gave, and what we took.

A wounded grouse dives toward the dreaming lake:
the moment vanishes, the memory lasts.
We wonder what we gave, and what we took.
Sorrow is long, silence accumulates.

The moment vanishes, the memory lasts.
Is there a reason why the grouse must die?
Sorrow is long, silence accumulates.
A yellow taxi drives across the sky.

Subway

We went down into the subway
and found a dead man on the tracks.
Nobody knew his name. We did not know
his address. He was not a man that any of us
had ever seen before. His face was familiar,
but we did not recognize
his eyes. He apologized for
being dead on the tracks; there was sorrow in his voice
when he apologized, a tone of unmistakable
regret.

The dead man had unimpressive hands.
He wore a brown suit, brown shoes,
brown socks, and had a brown moustache. His eyes
were grey. He looked to be about forty-nine—
a right age, someone said,
to be found dead on the tracks.

We put him on a table
and examined his teeth. His teeth
told us nothing. He was sorry for
the sparseness of information. "Forgive me," he said,
"for being dead—I never meant
to cause you any trouble." We studied him,
and probed, and searched, but came
to no conclusions. He shrugged.
He seemed to grieve a while, and then he spoke again,
a vague whisper, reciting from memory

long passages from *The Day of Doom.*
He closed his eyes
and hummed, tunelessly.

The third day after we found him
he began to scream. His screaming was unexpected.
It was the screaming of
a wild animal in a jungle: the cry of slow death
in a blue jungle that was webbed and tangled
with grotesque and unimaginable
forms of dying. We asked him to stop
but he didn't.

We put him in a box and sealed it tight.
We put the box inside a second box,
and still we heard his hateful noise. We carried him,
sealed in two boxes, far out to sea,
and dumped him over, without a prayer.

On overcast days, when we stand by the shore,
facing the wind, watching the waves as they
pound the sand, we hear him yet: his screaming
rises up from the deep water where we left him,
and the screaming we hear
is the piercing whine
of the iron wheels of a subway car,
screeching to a halt, too late,
in an emergency.

She Is Going to Be

She is going to be a small, single-engine aircraft
lost in the fog, looking for
a landing place
in a crowded city.

She will be a crippled Lithuanian soprano
singing the role of Mimi
in *La Bohème.* She is going to suffer, because suffering
is something she will be good at.

She will be left-handed, and she will never learn
how to play the piano. She will be
a telephone that rings and rings,
and nobody answers.

She will read the *Confessions* of St. Augustine
and will become interested in time, death,
remorse, love, and predestination. She will visit Carthage
and shop in the stores there.

She is going to have difficulty
with her orgasms—but she will practice
and she'll improve. She will plant herbs in flowerpots
on a windowledge in her kitchen.

She is going to be a secondhand Buick with bad brakes
driving slowly through heavy traffic.
She will be
heavy traffic.

At night, when she goes to sleep,
she will remove her feet, her eyes, and her breasts,
and she will put them under the bed
for safekeeping.

She will not know the names of famous Olympic athletes,
or the names of the Renaissance popes,
or the names of the makers of rare violins.
She will not remember who invented the cotton gin.

She is going to be an outdoor swimming pool
and strangers will swim in her. She will have
irregular menstrual periods. When she boards a bus,
she will not have the correct change.

She will have friends who die young,
and other friends who know about astrology, needlepoint,
and extrasensory perception. One of her neighbors
will make homemade sherry.

She will be angry, and she'll use foul words.
She'll fall in love, and she will be a slow freighter
moving in dense fog across quiet waters.
She will be, when necessary, a stained-glass window.

She is going to become pregnant.
She will think of birth as something vast and oceanic:
immense, large, complex, dangerous, frightening.
She will have the baby and put it up for adoption.

She will be snow when it snows, and rain
when it rains. She will be a city street
torn up and dug into. On weekends, she will be
a secondhand bookstore, with only herself to blame.

She will develop an interest in sky and clouds,
and she will learn all there is to learn
about heights, distances, and angles of elevation.
She will focus so intently on the sky

that she will leave the earth: rising, drifting.
Strangers will watch her through binoculars. She will go
far off, ascending slowly, moving toward a thick accumulation
of purple clouds.

Then she will fall. It happens
suddenly: she falls and falls, a lame weight
sinking through the wind. At the hospital
she will be dead on arrival.

They embalm what is left of her, repair
what they can. They put her in a clean dress.
In her coffin, she will be a garden of dead roses,
a garden of dead peonies, a garden of dead gardenias.

She will tell her friends, who come to look at her,
that she harbors no resentment.
"I am still a garden" she will explain, "even though
I'm in a state of ruin."

She will invite her friends, who come to visit her,
to linger for a while,
because there will still be much in her garden
to admire. They stay, walk through and browse,

touching her last, broken flowers. And then
they bury her, remembering her arms, her lips, her anger,
her dreams, her russet moods, and her fatal affection
for clouds.

We Have Lost Our Fathers

The sun goes down, we hide where we can.
We have all lost our fathers.
It is easier to dream
than not to dream. It is also easy
to fall out of a tree.

Sigmund Freud stood at a blackboard
writing sentences. He wrote
ninety-five sentences, and then stopped.
Karl Marx stopped. Julian Huxley stopped.
The Duke of Windsor went strolling in a park.

It is easy to sit in a boat and drift aimlessly,
letting the water take you. Water, water.
We go often to the well. We go often to the house
where nobody lives.

•

Franz Kafka peeled a carrot.
He cut it into seventeen pieces—
he ate sixteen of the seventeen pieces
and drank a glass of wine. He took
the seventeenth piece of the carrot he had peeled
and put it in an envelope. He put
a message in the envelope, saying THIS
IS THE CARROT OF THE LONG SORROW OF
OUR EXISTENCE. WE WILL DIE. THEY WILL

NOT REMEMBER
WHO WE WERE. He addressed the envelope
to his father, then put it in a bottom drawer
and never mailed it.

•

The sun goes down, we hide where we can.
It is easier to dream
than not to dream. We go often
to the well.
                    We go often to the house
where nobody lives.

Red

Red of sunsets, red of dying stars—
red birds, red horses,
red of the blood of the ones who were killed
by a terrorist bomb at Orly. Red earwigs,
red crabs. Red of lithium chloride.

We curse red: we need it
and seek it out. We dip our hands
in the blood of the past; we have not seen
the color of the future,
but when the future becomes the past
we know its mood
will be something that we recognize.

Red of disaster, red of upheaval and change.
Red of process, of things when they begin
and things when they end. Red Mars, red meteorites.
Red of red wine.
Red of the red grass of Gettysburg, where
more than 6000 died. Red moon,
red slaughter. Red pelicans raging in flight
over the waters of the Everglades. Red of lost dreams,
falling, burning.
Red of the last time we looked at the sun.
Red, invisible infrared,
of the middle of the night.

PART *2*

They

1

They take me, and open me
and empty me out. They leave nothing.
They peel my skin and hang it over a chair.
They take my feet, my hands,
my elbows. "Do you feel better now?" they ask.
"Are you satisfied?" They put me and my torn parts
in a drawer, where I won't
be found. They lock the drawer
and throw the key away. They walk off
and they remember me, from time to time,
as the busy one they have noticed
and put away for safe-keeping. I stay in the drawer
and remember them
as the bastards who broke my knees.

They with their dark eyes that are dark with
  the darkness of dark places,
and their tongues, which are sharpened steel.
Their slow nights, when the moon is a flat disc
  barely visible behind black clouds.
Their names, which are grey, and their stone intentions
                moving on iron wheels
  across an iron landscape.
Their expensive pens, and secret signatures.
Their velvet words that are
spoken softly, without emphasis:
    hushed tones, forbidden mysteries.

2

The gates open, and I go through.
They say: "Look how pale he is! How sick & lonely
he seems to be!" I go through into a place
where there are trees and cobblestones.
They say: "Are you sure you want to be here?"
The sky is dense: vibrant purple.
I eat a fig, some almonds. I hate this place:
this place is theirs. The sky is theirs,
and the cobblestones—
the figs and the almonds. Even the air
belongs to them.

They talk in a soothing voice,
saying: "Are you sorry you came?"
I don't turn back, because there is no place
to turn back to. I pass through the gates,
and through other gates, up a hill,
toward a grove of hemlocks that belong
to someone I don't know.

3

They want me! They want me!
They stand in a circle around me and say, "He's the one
  we were looking for!" They want me, they say.
They say my teeth are crooked and stained—they give me
    new teeth.
They say my eyes are too dark: they give me new eyes.
They want me, crowding around.
They need me, looking through a magnifying glass.
They touch me, saying: "He's a rock! A stone!
  A juniper! Let's send him to the moon!"
They want me blue, they want me green.
They want me like a tree in a garden.

They want me like a clear television picture
    carried from a far-off city.
They want me like a narrow waterfall
        tumbling down a steep gorge.
They need me: They take me and make me theirs.
They crave me and give me a new house, a new car,
    a new name, and new shoes.
They say: "Isn't he terriffic? Don't you like us now?"
I take my new shoes, and for a while I wear them.
They hurt my feet.

4

Sometimes, when they speak, I have the impression
they are really one: because their voices are one.
Their voices melt and merge, the way their faces merge,
dissolving to a single, stubborn force:
one mouth, one set of eyes, one chin,
and one firm voice, cajoling, persuading.

But there are days
when the wind blows right through that voice
and through that face
and the face falls apart into many faces
and the voice becomes
many voices, high and low,
male and female, all going at once,
scolding, laughing. I clap my hands over my ears
and run. The voices chase after me,
and I cut across the grass,
making for the far trees,
and hide myself
in a clump of wild raspberries, among thorns,
where the tangled faces
can't get near.

5

They have dreams, which they talk about.
There are no mountains in their dreams,
and no geysers. No lakes, no sunbaked canyons.
Their dreams are filled with thumbtacks and stale bread,
and letters they will never read.

They tell me to go downstairs
and I go down into a dim place
and stay a while. I go back up.
We meet on the stairs. Each of them has a face
like my face: lips like mine,
a nose like mine. They are not me.

I walk along and they walk in front of me
and behind me, to the left and the right of me.
They have legs and feet
like mine, and shoes like mine. I don't know who
they are.

6

They sucked the marrow from my bones,
and stole my eyes.
They nailed my tongue to a wall that was blue.
"Are you happy now?" they scoffed.
I wrote a long letter
objecting to the things they did.

A week passed. They turned up,
apologizing, with a basket of fruit.
I threw it in their face.

They sent a fifth of Jack Daniels.
I poured it down the sink.
They said: "He has such a temper!"
They went away and did not return.

Another week went by. I read in the paper
they had given me a citation
for the unusual courage I had shown
under trying circumstances.

7

"You miss the point," they say. "You have us
all wrong. What you don't grasp
is that we
are really
you!" I hear what they say,
and I think it over: that they,
their many heads, and many voices,
are one voice,
and the voice is mine. Me talking to me,
and me running away
from the things I say: the enemy I hide from
is myself.
            But if that's so
why did I nearly die
when they held me under water—
and why,
when they cut me open,
did I bleed?

They want me, they say. They still do want me!
Better than snow!
Better than blue sky after a thunderstorm!
They want me, but they're unsure.
They study me close: I'm not enough.
They want me, but they apologize: they made a mistake.
They take off my face,
erase my name.
They want me, they say,
but they also say: "He's no good for us!
We expected more!"

8

I stand in a place where there are no trees.
The sun is down.
I cannot see my father's face.
Darkness gathers near my feet.

If we move, we are wrong.
If we stand still, we are worse.
Who murdered me?
Who broke my bones?

They take & take
& I watch them
& listen. I am in this elevator again
going up
and down.

They say: "Go!"
And I go.
They say: "Stop!"
And I stop. It is always
the same.

"He wasn't so bad," they say. "We could
have lived with him, if he hadn't been
so stubborn. And so vile."

9

They come in the sky, and I am with them.
They find me, and I am alone.
They tell stories, and I am the story they tell.
They listen, and I explain who they are.
They walk away, and I follow.
They are restless, I lead them where they want to go.
They fall, and I fall with them.
They die, and in their death I find my life.
They live, and I teach them how to die.
They come back, and come back, and I am never free.

Afternoons bursting like thick, ripe grapes—
a whole summer of the warm, green life of grass.
Days of apricots and plums,
and always the moon, close and alive with light,
hovering above the trees. They are not the moon,
and they are nowhere in the sky—but if I go there,
to the trees, the moon, the sky, I know I will find them
where I never wanted
them to be.

They laugh, and they are the poison in my life.
They weep, and I am the knife that drives home.
They dig the earth, finding the emptiness
  of my dark name.
They move on, hiding, and I find them.
They try to escape, and they are mine.

PART *3*

Scenes of Violence

Scenes of violence, like great works of art,
make us pause. The knife goes in,
the body falls. The effect is lasting—
we carry it with us, as if the knife
had pierced not flesh merely,
a human life, but had cut deep
into a mystery we do not grasp
and dare not contemplate: as if
the knife had pierced a veil
concealing truths too terrible
to risk, and the blood that seeps through, staining
us, flows from
a place beyond the world we walk in,
a place we are not eager for,
a darkness possibly—and, for one moment,
when the knife goes in, we are forced to look,
and see. The moment is tense with an obscure clarity
in which everything
and nothing
is revealed.

Thomas Edison Considers the Past & the Future and Goes Off in Search of Something Else : : :

How the Titanic gets a big hole in it
and goes down. How the Shah of Iran
reclines on a couch and eats clams. How South Carolina
secedes from the Union. How Chiang Kai-shek
rents a Flying Tiger and goes to war. How Mae West,
cracking no smile, peels a grape. How the Angel Moroni,
sincerely gold, soars above Temple Square. Thomas Edison
complains to his assistant, Honest John Kruesi:
"It looks bad," he says, "but we will
work at it, pray at it, whistle, curse,
kick it to death if necessary—and it *will glow!*"
It did,
and still does. He filed the blueprint in a locker
in the basement of the Taj Mahal,
and then he ran off. He was last seen
disappearing in the blue steam of a fumarole
in Yellowstone National Park.

My Time

My time is my time. My time is slow,
it isn't what
it used to be. My time is sullen with dark eyes,
prowling through strange neighborhoods.

My time is the emptiness of broken hands,
and the emptiness of eyes that have
nothing to see, and the awkward emptiness
of the ones who die.

My time is an old car
parked on a high cliff. This car
has bad tires, bad brakes, bad rust, bad valves,
and bad intentions—

I stand behind this car
and push
it
over the edge.

My time like a broken thermometer!
My time like a bent spoon!
My time like a dead lightbulb!
My time like my time.

My time flows down from cold mountains,
finding its way into lakes and reservoirs.
I turn on a faucet in my house, and my time
gushes out: it wets my hands.

My time is water that I drink, and water
that I listen to, and water that
washes me, and water that flows away
in my urine.

My time is not my own. They take my time
and put their fingerprints
all over it. They grab my time and say
it belongs to them.

They soil my time with their clumsy hands,
and throw it back and forth—
I watch, and I am hopeless, because my time
is theirs.

My time is a brick wall that I
stop in front of. There is no ivy
on this wall; mortar is missing from the seams,
the bricks are cracked—

a spider crawls up the wall, approaching
the top. It hesitates, then comes
back down. My time is the spider
coming down off this wall—

it moves around in the gravel,
searching, probing; it enters a crevice
at the base of the wall
and disappears.

My time gathers in small rooms: it sits around
and waits. My time
prays for my enemies. My time
tells lies.

My time is left-handed and uncertain:
it walks and walks, wandering
in strange cities. It loses
its way—

falls down a manhole,
falls down a flight of stairs,
falls down a fire escape,
falls down an elevator shaft.

They pick up my time and write
ugly remarks all over it. Then they give it
back to me, I hold it in my hands. My time
is my time. It is never time enough.

Scuba Diver Found Dead in a Swamp

We're in the swamp again: mud, sedge,
marsh hawks circling and hovering—voles,
cypresses festooned with moss. The sun hangs overhead,
a blazing silver saucer. Things seem (somehow) wrong.

We dig down, and dig down, in dark, fertile mud
and find the body of a scuba diver
who was buried alive.
                                        This scuba diver
was someone we knew. We grew up with him.
He had blue eyes, a quick tongue, a broken nose,
a mouth filled with bad teeth.
All his life he had dreams that he would be
buried alive in a swamp,
and he was. He used to sing
in the shower. He owned a yellow Mercedes.
He read adventure novels and ate raw celery. One year
he vacationed in Switzerland, but he preferred
the Caribbean, where he dove for coral,
rare aquatic plants. One summer he filmed
two lobsters in the act of copulation.

The scuba diver's dead eyes stare out at us:
hard, gleaming gems. We feel uneasy
in the presence of these eyes: they are eyes that saw
life underwater
and death underwater, languid struggles
won and lost. We don't know how
he got to be where he is. His wild eyes

fix us in an unnerving stare, as if we were the ones
who put him there. Maybe we are. We see in his eyes
the terror and the primal fear
of his underwater gardens: turtles, sea snakes,
algae, slime—they are not eyes
that we can gaze at long. We cover them with mud
and move on, through acres of tall sedge, slow,
under a hot sun, making our way
toward higher ground.

Everything Humanly Possible Was Tried and We Failed % % % % % % % % % %

We tried apples, teeth, and pliers,
but nothing worked. We tried
a snowplow and a portable radio. Glazed apricots
were of no use at all. We tried billiard balls
and five gold rings. No one can say we did not do our best.
We tried remembering and forgetting,
and suede shoes, swans, an upright piano.
We resorted to bifocals and original sin.
The *Encyclopedia Americana* was of no avail.
Water from Lourdes was ineffectual.
We grew used to the fact that we would never accomplish
what we had set out to do. We used pewter candlesticks
and reinforced concrete. Why, and why,
and when, and when—it was difficult
to understand. We wondered if a stone would help,
or a novel by Defoe. We listened to Mahler,
and Monteverdi. It was still bad: formless, vague,
not finished. Therefore we tried again,
and do, and did,
and still we are busy, wondering where to turn next,
and how . . . wondering if a Ming vase,
or a Leica, or a stove,
or a dwarf,
or a new roof,
or an octopus,
or a cherry tree . . .

Forbidden Fruit

It was a purple river, and we knew how to sail it:
with a rifle in the bottom of the canoe,
and a sharp eye for alligators.
There were natives on the banks, naked,
holding spears and blowpipes. We survived the natives,
but the animals were something else,
barking and screeching in the hot sun
until the sun itself was an animal
opening its jaws. We dipped our hats
in the purple water
and drank—it was the only water
we had.

Near the source of the river, in a grove of trees,
we found what we were looking for—
a broken temple, ancient, overgrown,
adorned with pineapples made of gold.
There were no natives here
and no animals. The silence
was like the heat, implacable. We touched the gold,
trembling as we held it, feeling
a sudden fear, a strange commingling
of terror and delight: we took what we could,
loading the canoe
with all it could carry. Then we stretched out
and rested in the grass. We could not sleep.
The sun raged, an angry copper bird.
Our minds were ablaze
with a strange and alien fever.

As we readied ourselves for the trip back,
we thought again about the river—
the blowpipes, alligators, the stabbing sun.
The turquoise sky was dangerous with vultures.
Standing there, eager to go, we lingered
and understood. There was no getting back.
The gods of the place
were against us—
our lives
as worthless as stone.

We unloaded the gold pineapples,
replacing them, one by one,
where we had found them, in a neat row.
We lingered on the steps of the temple.
The silence, now, was weirdly audible, like music.
The trees were still, the sky an awesome bronze.
We slept there, dreaming of home. It was an easy sleep,
we could ask for none better.

The trip downstream was swifter than we expected,
but fraught with troubles. Twice we capsized,
the rapids nearly killed us.
Worst of all were the nights, the maddening susurrus
of crickets and frogs. There was no comfort in the dark,
only a sense of being suffocated
in folds of black velvet. The natives were invisible,
chirping their signals from tree to tree.

We made it back, but the world we came home to
was strangely different—smaller, claustrophobic;
its geography had shrunk. We grew old here,
with the memory of our journey always haunting us,
coming back in nightmares.
We had beaten the river, there was comfort in that.
But the gods of the temple had been too stern.

There were thoughts of returning,
and often there were plans,
but our plans grew old with our bodies,
and finally there was only the recollection—
the gold in the shape of pineapples,
and the weight of it, the burden,
which is always with us.

I'll Leave at Two

I'll leave at two. They'll try
to stop me, hold me back.
They'll say: "Don't dare go!"
But I will. They'll block my way.

We'll talk, argue. I'll leave
at two. They'll tell me not
to go. They'll say it's better if
I stay. Delay?

I'll leave at two, and when they stop me
I'll insist. They have their ways,
their stone persuasion. I can be stubborn
too.

I'll make to leave, and they will
stop me at the door. They won't apologize.
One of those days, dim and unpleasant—
a wrong afternoon.

I'll leave at two, and they'll back
off. What can they do? They'll move
aside, and I'll go through and out.
It will be over.

Or they'll resist, not let me pass,
strike out until I fall—
punch, kick,
leave me numb.

I'll leave at two. I see murder in
their eyes. They hover by the door
and don't apologize. And now it's time:
I move to go.

Joan of Arc Responds to the Grand Inquisitor, Explaining Who She Is : : : : : :

I am not an oriental rug or a xerox copier.
I am not September.
I am not an aspirin, or a credit card,
 or an unfinished symphony in the key of B minor.
I am not a field of wheat waiting for the harvest.
A cargo ship in the North Atlantic, sending out an SOS—
 the ship goes down, nobody is saved; wreckage is
  spotted by a searchplane, but the crew is lost: no
 hope, no rescue, they never had a chance; it's a
  black, mean day . . . I am not that ship!
I am not a forgery, a counterfeit, a bad check, a worm.
I am not a bargain basement.

I want to live in a house in a tree: the floors are
 red velvet, strawberries grow in the living room,
  grapes on the walls.
So many things: I am not . . . I am . . . am not . . .
A blue memory on a green day. A bowl of flowers.
 A box of silverware sold at auction.
A soft dream, a name forgotten.
A cancelled postage stamp.
A free brochure.

We have walked a long distance.
I am not a road sign or a Douay-Rheims bible.
Apple blossoms!
Orange hollyhocks!
I am not my knees, my nose, my ankles, my eyes.

A forest in a dry season: someone drops a match,
  the forest goes up in flames. Black bones of charred trees,
  miles and miles. . . I am not that ruined forest!
Confusion spreads.
Inner turmoil.
A slow mood, crouched, cat-like, waiting in the dark.
Violent and soft: blue, implausible.
I am not a desert or a stone.

Saying No

Harry Blorr was forty-two years old, with a wife
and three kids, one house, one car,
and three heads on his shoulders.
He said: "Life is awful!"
He said: "I don't want to live!"
He hated his wife and hated his kids,
and one of his heads (the one with green hair)
was total embarrassment: it said
unpleasant things. Harry Blorr
considered divorce
but couldn't afford it, and considered suicide
but found it
unattractive. He advertised for a mistress
but could not find one with three heads to
match his three heads—so he
went off to New Mexico
and built a house equipped with solar heat
and a windmill,
and studied painting. His three heads
painted three pictures at a time:
three snails, & three clocks, & three slender girls
each with three vaginas. Then he turned
to self-portraiture: he was three dark selves
with three flaming mouths. "There is no
future," he said, when he saw
the terror he had painted in his eyes, "—no hope and
no resurrection!" He drove off,
drove and drove, until he ran out of gas,
and found his vocation, at long last, as a missing
person.

They Tell Me the Emptiness

They tell me the emptiness of empty places—
empty tenements, empty cellars,
the emptiness of barrels that have been drained
and left to dry out in the sun, and boxes
that have been opened and thrown away,
and old books that have been read and reread
until there is nothing left inside them.

They talk of the emptiness of clouds
after the clouds have let go of their rain,
and stones that are heavy with their own emptiness,
I cannot lift them. There is an emptiness that lingers
after things have been packed and carried off,
the way a house is empty
after the moving van has pulled away.

They tell me the emptiness of trawlers lost at sea,
and of planes that crash against mountains
and burn, until even their emptiness is on fire.
The fatigue of blighted trees,
rivers when they are dry, dead grass,
dead dogs, dead worms,
dead cattle.

They tell me the emptiness of my own going,
and I am slow to listen, because of all the emptiness
it is the worst and longest, a lonesome emptiness
I do not want to hear: how I am empty,

the sky is empty, and the earth I dig is empty,
and my hands are burdened with a growing emptiness
that won't be filled.

I walk through the amber silence of my slow days,
gathering bits and pieces
of all the emptiness I find: open fields, wide streets,
autumn trees, leaves heaped and burning,
and the limpid eyes of my four children who
look on, inquisitive, gazing through my emptiness
toward the dark and dreamless rhythm of the sea.

The Camel

One day a camel turned up
on Francis Lewis Boulevard. It stopped traffic.
It was not a camel that had
escaped from a zoo: it was a camel that was

authentic and new, a true camel that had materialized
out of thin air. We liked the camel.
It was blind in one eye and needed help. We fed it
and kept it warm.

One day the camel passed
through the eye of a needle. We were startled—glad.
The camel was pleased with itself.
"I have arrived," it said.

We brought the camel gifts: gold,
scented soap, myrrh. We also brought
other things. The camel didn't know
what to do with the myrrh.

The camel was more special
than we had imagined: it gave meaning
to our lives. Without the camel we would not have become
the persons we are.

One afternoon the camel announced
it would remain with us no longer.
We pleaded with it to stay, but nothing we said
could make it change its mind.

Suddenly, the camel was gone—only its eye
remained, its one good eye
hovering in the air: intense, dark,
a lonely orb. We knelt before it

and prayed: *Save us from disaster!*
Save us from ourselves! The eye
gazed at us with deep compassion.
It winked, and disappeared.

We feel peculiar without the camel in our midst:
desolate, forlorn. Yet we feel, strangely,
that the camel is somehow in touch, watching over,
presiding—

the camel with its hump, its fleshy lips, thick tongue,
horny callosities, two-toed feet,
and its memories of the traffic that stood still
on Francis Lewis Boulevard.

One day, we recall, the camel, in a state of boredom,
stood up and danced—nothing sensational, a common waltz,
but a waltz performed with an ease and a grace
we had not seen before.

All the meaning of the camel, we realized,
was in that dance. We caught it on film.
On bad days, rain, dark moods, we turn out the lights
and roll the film. The camel's there again—dancing,

moving gracefully. We feel the power, the slow joy.
We stand up out of our chairs and move toward
the shadows on the screen: we enter the shadows
and join the dance, feeling the life, the death, the dread,

the bliss, the inexplicable lift. We go on dancing
until the music fades
and the camel winks–
and, despite ourselves, we disappear.

Pantoum of the Broken Door

We gained entry by breaking down the door.
We killed the king, the prince, and 2 lords attendant.
We raped the queen.
We said: "No matter, we always knew she was a whore!"

We killed the king, the prince, and 2 lords attendant.
The queen screamed bloody murder.
We shrugged. "No matter, we always knew she was a whore!"
We grabbed the gold plate and the candlesticks.

The queen screamed bloody murder:
we left her raging, black-and-blue.
We took the gold plate and the candlesticks
and buried them, for safe-keeping, in an orchard.

The queen raged on, she was black-and-blue.
We took her jewels and her diadem,
and buried them, in dark soil, in an orchard.
In calmer days, we'll dig them up again.

We took the jewels, and took the diadem.
We raped the queen.
In calmer days, we may go back again.
We got in by smashing down the door.

Policemen's Ball

The police arrive, playing blue harmonicas.
They sing and play
and also dance. The police with dark, sunburned brows
and blue harmonicas
arrive, throwing chrysanthemums in the air—
it is not easy
to be a blue chrysanthemum
or a harmonica
at a policemen's ball. The police with sudden eyes
and slow chrysanthemums
sing and dance
and play: a brown mood unpeels from their smiles.
They sign their names on the wall
and leave their fingerprints. They tell stories
and travel back and forth
through a vague field
of blind chrysanthemums. They sing,
and dance, and form a circle,
moving slowly
around a corpse on a table: they throw
chrysanthemums. It is not easy
to be a blue corpse on a table, packed in ice,
at a policemen's ball. The corpse grieves,
listening to the blue harmonicas. The police hold hands,
moving in a circle. And now they touch this corpse—

touch feet, and knees, and genitals. They praise
this corpse, and honor it,
an authentic, well-paid American corpse.
The corpse dreams on, reminiscing,
regretting, sinking slowly
in a blue field of dead chrysanthemums
at the policemen's ball.

PART *4*

Cloud

A blue cloud settles down
near the house where you live. You admire it:
its blurred, amorphous quality.
You like the way it spreads out, loose and easy,
in all directions.
                    Inside the cloud
you find things: a fig,
a spoon, a tooth. You find an old, worn photograph
of yourself when you were six. You walk along, casually,
and you come upon George Washington
in an orchard. He sits alone
on a high ledge of rock, counting his trees.
His face has a bland, abstract quality,
the face of an accountant
working overtime.
                    You walk on
through the dim acres of the cloud—it's bigger (vaster)
than you imagined. In a far corner
you see a dancer: naked, moving slowly,
a dull loneliness in her eyes.
In another corner you find a plastic replica
of Jesus crucified. The replica bleeds,
real blood. You go on walking
and you see things you had hoped
never to see: smashed cars, bruised corpses,
dead animals, a bombed-out city. It crosses your mind
that this cloud
is no dream, and it is
nothing new.
                You've been in this cloud

longer than you can remember, and you can't
get out. You go down
a flight of marble stairs, across grass,
still in the cloud, and after much walking,
much groping, you stumble upon
the Battle of Bull Run, where they are still slugging it out
with sabers, and carbines, and cannon, and grapeshot,
and charging cavalry, and you barely escape
with your life.

Through the Window

He had something else on his mind—
he wasn't thinking stones, or newspapers, or lilacs.
He was dreaming something vague, insubstantial.
It was there, hanging before him, though he couldn't
give it a name. Was it a tree?
A moving cloud?

I want, he thought. *I want* . . .
It rushed upon him, a sudden incandescence,
neither male nor female,
richly neuter, with a flash of danger in its eyes—
a green desire which, even in his yearning for it,
filled him with something he recognized as fear.
Is this death, he wondered. Is this
the improbable way it arrives?

He saw, then, through the window,
it was a common day—drab, cold November.
He saw a tree, black naked branches,
and a dog romping.
And still it hung before him—fading,
less vivid than before,
inviting him into a drowsy silence
which still he wanted,
and still he loathed. He turned away, deriving comfort
from the objects in the room. This is a rug,
this is a chair, this a vase, and this
a photograph. And yet—
fading, less insistent than before: *this*
is . . . this is . . .

When You Say Yes

A crash landing in Uganda, in the mouth of
   a diamond mine, is not more exciting than your eyes
   when you say yes. When you say yes,
it's an emergency of sorts. The police arrive,
fire engines scream into position.
You could be a whole department store on fire.
The customers panic, desperate to get out.
Not all of them do.

When you say yes, it's a tree crashing down on
somebody's roof: the tree smashes right through
and traps two people in bed
who aren't supposed
to be in bed together. It's the furnace
breaking down, and the stove not working,
and all the windows shattering,
letting the wind blow through. An earthquake
is not more dangerous; a bomb shelter
is no protection at all.

When you say yes it's better than
an air raid over Berlin in 1944—and bolder,
wilder, than a commando attack deep in the heart
of enemy territory, filmed in technicolor.
But O, love, beautiful as you are,
do not ask me, please, to be the cameraman
when the munitions factory blows—and I refuse,

firmly and forever refuse, to be the one who gets killed
when the railroad station burns
and the rushing locomotive
runs off the track.

Mud

Mud and the madness of mud: dirt roads,
autumn rain, swamps, lowlying fields. Green mud
at the bottom of silver lakes. Soft mud,
slow mud . . . mud the body turns into.

Mud that was bones and fingers, and mud
that was the heart. Mud of the eye, the tooth,
the palate. Mud of the lip and tongue.
Mud in which (dangerously) we begin.

Mud of our memories, lost dreams. Anger of mud,
sorrow of mud.
Mud that we wash off, cleansing ourselves
under a warm sun, near a waterfall.

Mud of our mothers who have died, and our fathers
who also died. Mud that never talks.
Mud that we stare at, wondering if it is only mud.
Mud that we enter & make a home in, losing our names.

Mud in which we move, and thrive, and grow, and die,
and begin again. Mud where we search and probe,
terrified, looking for the ungathered meaning
of our lives.

Litany

God of grass, God of roses
Have mercy on our allergic noses
Pity our bronchial wheezes
God of Adam, God of Jesus
God of Abraham, God of Moses
Deodorize our halitosis
Lord of all creation
Relieve us of our constipation
God of depths, God of voids
Take away our hemorrhoids
God of sempiternal session
Tranquilize our manic depression
God of da Vinci and della Robbia
Ventilate our claustrophobia
God of transcendental rumors
Take pity on our malignant tumors
God of canticles, God of psalms
Sing louder than our atom bombs
God of underprivileged nations
Look kindly on our fornications.

From blowouts on the highway
Lord deliver us
From headaches at the movies
Lord deliver us
From mosquitoes buzzing in our ears at night
Lord deliver us
From flu, grippe, mumps, and measles
Lord deliver us

From poisonous cranberry sauce
    Lord deliver us
From botulous tuna fish
    Lord deliver us
From drought that dries up our gardens
    Lord deliver us
From the green glare of desire
    Lord deliver us
From the purple throb of memory
    Spare us, O Lord

God of the knots in shoelaces
Have mercy on us who curse the knots
                & tear at the laces.

Numerology

One slams the door, two frowns.
Three rolls around on the floor. Four hides.
Five runs away and is never seen again.
Six masturbates.
Seven falls down a flight of stairs.
Eight sits by a window and sees
an old man walking a dog. Nine sneezes.
Ten slams the door
and adds nothing.

Two is the one with a moustache.
We saw two in the barbershop, getting
a trim. Two never became famous, never did
anything special . . . planted no trees, built no houses,
burned no bridges. Two died of complications arising
out of a bout with the flu. The funeral of two
was poorly attended. He was remembered,
mainly, as a man who paid a barber
to trim his moustache.

One for the mountain, one for the morgue.
One for the rain
and the lingering blue sorrow
of our days. One for the nose, and one for the heart,
and one for the tongue, and one for the liver, and one
for the spleen. One for the dream
from which we awake, knowing it was only
a dream. One for the one
who pays.

Seven buys a gun and kills an antelope—
kills a swan, then an elephant.
Kills a whole flock of bluebirds,
steps on a worm. Robs a bank in Pasadena
and shoots a guard, then races off
in a red Honda and is not seen again for
seven days. Seven is hunted down for killing
an orphan, a nurse, a cop, a cabby, a dentist, a priest,
and the Secretary of the Interior.

Three is a gift of trees: birds singing,
clouds pasted on a blue sky. Three
rides a motorcycle through Minnesota
and stops at a bar—tells stories,
laughs with the locals, eats a ham sandwich,
a pickle. Three is famous with the girls,
but drinks too much, a weakness for lager—
turns rowdy, tears up a storm. Three
is a crowd.

Four is the one that never moves.
Four sits in a chair
and watches TV. Reads a newspaper
in a chair, hums a tune
in a chair, blows his nose
in a chair, plays the stockmarket
in a chair, eats broccoli
in a chair. Four wonders why anyone
would ever want to go to the moon.

Six doesn't know what to do next. She's been
a waitress, a maid, a part-time librarian,
and a checkout girl at Caldor's.
She tries her hand as a hooker, but never
gets the hang of it. She takes up dancing
and lands a job in an east-side bar. Night after night
she moves, sways: bone and flesh oozing in a warm,
sensual flow. She's bored, tired.
Restless. She moves to Hoboken and changes her name.

Nine is lean and tall, thinking lofty thoughts:
thinking things will change, improve. They do,
but slowly. Thinking things will transmogrify—
thinking, perhaps, a revolution. Reads Marx,
studies the life of Che Guevara; delves into Mao,
Ho, Lenin. After eight tense months in the
42nd Street Library, nine undergoes a change of heart
and takes a job
in a bank.

One slams the door, two goes home.
Three gets high on gin. Four watches a bank heist
on television. Five stays in hiding
and is not seen again. Six stands on a stage
and takes off her clothes. Seven hijacks a submarine.
Eight eats a banana cream pie.
Nine plants a bomb
in the Chase Manhattan. Ten slams the door
and adds nothing.

This Strange Confusion

There was an old lady for sale
on Morningside Heights. I drove over
and checked her out. She had old eyes,
an old nose, old teeth,
and an old liver. "I may not be much,"
she granted, "but I still have some life in me."
I bought her and brought her home.
I hung her arms and legs in a closet.
I put her head on a shelf in the kitchen.
I left her torso in the living room.
"I seem to be in many parts," she observed,
"and in many different places. I do enjoy
this strange confusion!"

We lived together for three months,
then I grew tired of her. I put an ad
in the paper. She objected. "I'm fed up," she said
"with being bought and sold. I've had enough.
Put me back together, please, and turn me loose!"
I turned her loose. I took her arms and legs
out of the closet, and put her head
back on her shoulders. "It wasn't bad,"she shrugged,
"while it lasted. I hope we never
meet again." The last I saw of her
she was walking up the block,
past the supermarket—old, disheveled,
but with a saucy spring in her step
that gave me second thoughts.

Praise for Famous Explorers

It is permitted to give thanks
for famous explorers—

F. Drake finding his way
around
the evil horn

Sir Walter R. whose head
came off

Cortes who did
Montezuma
in

and many homesick sailors
who died of scurvy.

They are going off again
to some
blue moon,

others to
the bottom of the sea—

and some are searching
the dim interior
of the atom   where unstable mesons

huddle
like frightened aborigines, planning

a counter-
attack. See how these mesons
clench their fists:

they will have (perhaps)
their way?

A Vast Silence Arrives in the Sky in the Shape of a Phantom Battleship

This vast silence arriving in the sky
like a grey battleship
is a silence we were waiting for. We knew it would come
sooner or later. We look at it
and snap its picture.
                                        This battleship
with smokestacks and armor plate
rides among the clouds. It survived
the Sea of Japan. It was hit
by torpedoes and artillery. Ninety-eight men
died on this ship, hundreds were wounded.
It sank nine enemy cruisers
and a submarine; it fired from offshore
and destroyed a city. Now it comes in the clouds,
in the shape of a vast silence.
We televise its arrival, and drink
a toast: *To the phantom battleship in the sky!*
To the clouds! To the sun!
To the grey silence! To the ones who died!
To the ones who had the bad luck not to die!
To the sunk cruisers! To the ruined city!
To the sunk submarine!

The quiet battleship takes its place
among the clouds: it does not move. It seems content
to be where it is. It has memories, but no regrets.
It spends its time listening to the echoes
of the battles it came through. It looks
the worse for wear. The sun passes over it,

and for a time
the sun is gone—we're in the shadow
of this battleship, in the grip
of its unnerving silence. This awesome silence
anchored in the sky
in the grey shape of a battleship: it hangs there,
motionless, guarding its secrets
and its dead.

Getaway

Getting away from the scene of the crime
is not always easy. The car doesn't start–
or, before you reach the car,
somebody's mother, buxom, loaded with packages,
blocks your way and you both go sprawling.
Shots are fired, you're nearly killed. But you
slip through: you mix with the crowd
and hurry along
to a diner
where you order
a bowl of soup. It's bad luck.
The waitress notices dry blood, somebody else's,
on the back of your hand. You notice
that she notices: and she notices
you noticing. She drops the soup and screams,
and you want to scream back, an ugly hellish scream
that will obliterate her scream, and maybe her.
But there is nothing you can do,
only turn and run again, into the crowd,
toward another diner, in another city,
and another waitress, somewhere, and hope she will
look at your stained hands, touching them,
and not care.

A Purple Silence

He dreams of islands in the sun, white beaches
beaten by warm waves, and towering palms
that lean against the sky, green apparitions.
Naked girls approach him, bearing white
chrysanthemums, and plums on silver platters.
Their breasts, immense and brown, sway softly.
What better world? What better place? These women
coming near . . . to lie down into them,
into their warm, into their soft, and then
to wake from them as from a lingering dream.

He does not want to read another book.
It would be simpler, kinder, if the wisdom
of the ages could be taken in
like food—or sipped, a rare, exotic wine.
And what is wisdom anyway? Has it
ever slowed the oiled machinery
of war, or stopped the hunger of the poor?
The disappointment that he feels is an
old emptiness he has been gathering
and storing up, the gaping hole of all
his lingering questions: unaccounted for,
unanswered. He names this emptiness, where all
his doubts accumulate, *A Purple Silence*
Where the Porpoises Forget Their Dreams.

What can it mean, this sudden restlessness—
these poplars shivering in the wind, these crows
black and barking in an amber sky?
An awesome terror reaches him, from long

ago, out of the first small life that drifted
in the sea: he does not want to die.
It would be easier to be a wave
disappearing in the ocean, or
a cloud disintegrating into rain.
To have been part of history, conscious,
counting the years—this is the ache he feels,
the source of a malingering remorse
which he will never solve or comprehend.
What difference can it make? Who notices?

The mailman drops the mail, the dog barks.
He mixes another cup of instant coffee.
This is home, he knows no other place.
And still the dream burns on, intangible
but real—the palms, the warming breeze, the sun,
and the brown approaching women, whose arms are filled
with promises. They will not disappoint.
Their presence is a hushed and gathering silence
arriving from the other side of sleep.
Ageless, they are forever drawing near,
with dark, mysterious smiles, and sullen eyes . . .
the evanescent motion of the sea.

About the Author—

Nicholas Rinaldi teaches literature and creative writing at Fairfield University, where he also directs the Writing Program. His poems, articles, and short stories have appeared widely in such journals as *The Yale Review, New American Review, Mississippi Review, Southwest Review*, and in many other quarterlies and reviews. His first collection of poems, *The Resurrection of the Snails*, was published by Blair in 1977, and he has presented readings of his poetry in numerous colleges and museums across the country. He resides in Connecticut with his wife, Jacqueline.